Unbelievers

Also by John Mateer

Poetry

Burning Swans
The Civic Poems
Anachronism
(Echo)
Spitting Out Seeds
Mister! Mister! Mister!
Barefoot Speech
Loanwords
Makwerekwere
The Ancient Capital of Images/Imaji no Koto
The Brewery Site: Six Poems
Words in the Mouth of a Holy Ghost
Southern Barbarians
The Republic of the East
Elsewhere
The Travels/Viagens
Ex-white/Einmal-weiss: South African Poems
The Azanians
The West: Australian Poems 1989-2009
This Dark Book/Este Livro Escuro

Prose

Semar's Cave: an Indonesian Journal

John Mateer

Unbelievers,
or
'The Moor'

Shearsman Books

First published in the United Kingdom in 2013 by
Shearsman Books
50 Westons Hill Drive
Emersons Green
BRISTOL BS16 7DF

Shearsman Books Ltd Registered Office
30–31 St. James Place, Mangotsfield, Bristol BS16 9JB
(this address not for correspondence)

www.shearsman.com

ISBN 978-1-84861-281-5

Copyright © John Mateer, 2013.
The right of John Mateer to be identified as the author of this work has been asserted by him in accordance with the Copyrights, Designs and Patents Act of 1988. All rights reserved.

Acknowledgements

Some of the poems have previously appeared, either solely in the original English or with/in translation, in the following magazines: *PEN International* (UK), *World Literature Today* (USA), *Jacket2* (USA/web), *Criatura* (Portugal), *La Traductière* (France), *Lyrik Vannen* (Sweden), *Shearsman* (UK), *Poetry Salzburg* (Austria). My thanks to the editors and the translators Jacques Rancourt, Inês Dias, Jonas Ellerström. As well, larger suites of the poems have appeared in the booklet, *The Language*, with Farsi translation by Layli Rahksha, and the selection, *Antologia Breve* (Lingua Morte), translated by Miguel Martins, and the broadsheet collection, *The Azanians* (T41, Lisbon).

The poet would like to thank the Municipality of Idanha-a-Nova, the Dean's Office of the Faculty of Letters and the Rectory of the University of Coimbra for a residency in the village of Monsanto, Portugal; and, for its residency, El Gouna, Egypt. He is grateful to the Department for Culture and the Arts of Western Australia for two travel grants and a project grant.

He would also like to acknowledge the following people who at various points and in various ways helped with the writing: (in Australia) Ali Alizadeh, Layli Rakhsha; (in Portugal) Andreia Sarabando, Miguel Martins, Luis Mitras, Inês Dias, Roger Meintjies, Angela Ferreira and Graça Capinha; (in Macau) Carlos Morais José; (in Slovenia) Marjan Stojan; (in Egypt) Mohamad Metwalli, Ahmad Taha, Sameer Abu Masry; and (in many places) Mónica Estèves Alonso.

The last line of the poem-sequence '(Twelve Poems)' is from Peter Cole's translation of Avraham Ben Yitzhak, published in *Collected Poems* (Jerusalem: Ibis Editions, 2003). The poem 'Yuhanna Al-Armani, the Coptic Painter' is based on the research of Magdi Guirguis in his book *An Armenian Artist in Ottoman Cairo: Yuhanna al-Armani and his Coptic Icons* (Cairo: American University in Cairo Press, 2008).

Contents

The Mall

11 Mall of the Emirates

Al'Andalus

15 After the only known poem by Al' Rahman
16 The Books
17 The West
18 For Ibn Battuta
19 While in the Salon…
20 Images of the Saint
22 (Kaffir)
23 The Andalusian Poet
28 Sé, Coimbra
29 That Proverb
30 The Moor
31 Ghazal
32 João
34 Cide Hamete Benegeli…
35 Graffiti, Lavapies
36 Alfama

37 ### The Language

Azanians

53 The Auteur
54 When he suggested…
55 Self-Portrait as a Camel conjured by Daemons
56 Question for António Damásio
57 Ghosts
58 Corpus
59 What should, perhaps, be corrected
60 Africans

61	Her Experience
62	Fathers
63	La Nacão
64	Virgem do Leite
65	The Drowning of Bahadar Shah
66	Ekphrasis
67	The Hotel
68	Sunday Night at Teatro A Barraca
69	Pessanha's House
70	Homage
71	Coimbra
72	Poesia Incompleta
74	Fado
75	Poet without Qualities
76	Documents
77	This Era
78	"My House is Empty"
79	An Acquaintance

Os Elefantes Brancos

83	The Ex-Photographer
89	The Translator

95	**Monsanto**

119	**(Twelve Poems)**

Meydan

133	'Medan'
134	The Ayrian face of Nefertiti
135	The Copts
136	"We are all Kahlid Said"
137	The Translator and the Poets
139	Six Months After the Revolution
140	Winsor Hotel

141	Cats of Zamalek
142	Their Donkey
143	On the way to an Oasis…
144	Resident
145	The Nigerian Novelist
146	At Twilight
147	St Anthony's Cave
148	Valley of the Kings
149	Ode
150	Red Sea
151	This is not a Land that is Seen

The Bridge

| 155 | Yuhanna Al'Armani, the Coptic Painter |
| 156 | On Galata Bridge |

Afterword

| 159 | Echolalia, or an Interview with a Ghost |

Half of man is his tongue, and half his heart.
—The Poem of Zuhayr
Eighth Century A.D.

The Mall

Mall of the Emirates

We don't use the word "exile" anymore,
despite meeting in the Mall of the Emirates,
that hyperbolic cave, ordering what is expensive
peasant food, while contemplating our prospects
on two or, maybe, three continents,
confessing that we no longer return to our natal countries.
We're unlike our taxi-drivers, with our perpetually
renewable visas and self-conscious amnesia,
even if we, too, could forever cruise down Dubai's freeways,
reminiscing on the stupas of Anuradapura,
how in the sunlight they glint like ricebowls over-turned.
In consolation we have what used to be Literature,
its metamorphosis, those phantoms, our other lives.
Or isn't it the other way round? Haven't we been expelled
from the Garden of Nothingness to wander, life-long,
lost in thought, imagining Al Muteena Street as an avenue in Tunis,
grey palmtrees attempting shadow against gilded exhaust haze?
Ali, remember that dream you told me of: Hafiz
appearing to an Australian scholar, nominating him
his Interpreter? That's probably how we ended up here
in this extravaganza of shops, this oasis,
as a poem born on the tip of another's tongue,
as perfectly translatable synonyms for that word: "exile".

Al'Andalus

After the Only Known Poem by Abd Al' Rahman

The palm-tree I beheld in far Westralia,
far from what might be called its origin, far from things familiar.
I shouted: *You and I are far away, in a weird place among strangers!*
I have been away from home so long nobody knows me, nowhere!
You, too, have grown up in a world where you are still called a stranger.
You: refugee, foreigner, exile, Unbeliever! Stranger,
know that there are now so many of us—reincarnated nobodies—everywhere.
May someone one day say that we weren't merely illegals, wanderers.
May we someday be discovered somewhere far away, far away from this
        Westralia.

The Books

Not all the books were thrown on the bonfires.
Some, as Ibn Zunbul recounts, were stored in abandoned mosques.
Our Traveller, hearing of this, was led to a mosque,
and through the keyhole saw nothing,
but heard—not wind—the rustle of worms.
Maybe, he thought, *all books are the Uncreated?*

The West
—Graffiti for the ruins of Córdoba Cathedral

Here, in this unreconstructed mosque,
the arches and proliferating pillars
are a million stilled camels returning
to the Caliphate of the Invisible,
leaving us behind, here, in this emptied
mosque of Mind.

For Ibn Battuta

      I have sought
your Spirit here in scorching
      Andalusia. But only found
those memories
      of my travels, that
Shunyata.

While in the Salón dos Embajadores
—Remembering Years Ago Lecturing in Australia on 'The Poem' in the Second Week of September 2001

The New Capitalist students had been shouting at the Feral
who'd come to "drum up support" for a manifestation.

I'd begun with the words of Adonis, his "Dream of New York",
its exploding skyscrapers and wingéd people floating like swallows.

    Their unadulterated silence spoke:

We are only ever marginalia, never a poetics of Terror…

Images of the Saint

On the Painting

Neither that album page, nor its pristine miniature painting
of a fabled Persian garden where plants bloom with human features,
nor that monochromatic landscape in Coetzee's *Age of Iron*
under which, as under a bloodied Oriental carpet,
there were the dead faces none of us could avoid stepping on,

this panel of the Altar of the Virgin of the Navigators in the Real Alcázar,
in the chamber from which Queen Isobel despatched the Conquistadors,
she who like the Eternal Mother harboured all behind her chador,
this statement on the Expulsion of the Moors—

> *Santiago on a white horse, sword raised and poised, ready to swoop;*
> *the heads of the disembodied, their faces stony and sprouting from the ground.*

ON THE STATUE

When in the Cathedral at Santiago de Compostela I will be invited
to hug, for good luck, the marble torso of the Saint,
I won't. Not for moral reasons.

Embracing someone from behind like that
reminds me too much of how, in the Apartheid army,
we were taught to approach the enemy,

to slit the throat.

(Kaffir)

Mirror.

The Andalusian Poet

Quartet of Echoes

That poem
        of his
landscape
        is yours
and mine.

     Whose voice?

Of that play
all I remember
are those women,

like wraiths,
like the black-garbed
sisters

of Our Poet,
flocking around
him for the ghost

of a photo.

My singing is yours—

At his birthday
fireworks display,
the Poet doesn't
know who he is:

    In your prison-cell
you echoed that.

(Reprise)

Doves of my youth!

You seemed to be there
in a lovely park in Madrid
staring down through the leaves
at the cute tanning tourists

Doves of my youth!

Memories of my first garden,
that happy forest hidden deep
in the goldmine of my heart
where even we can't be lost

Doves of my youth!

You seemed to be there
in a park in summery Madrid,
but only I was heard
there, perched among you,

Doves of my youth!

Sé, Coimbra

Rivers of rocks running under my feet are streets,
and the weathered buildings my shadows skim
are photo-ready, after the fact, *this*:

that I look and look for the stone-mason's words
engraved on the Cathedral, a Moor's utterance
that could translate as:

…easier to change faith than re-hew stone.

That Proverb

Remember that photograph we saw
        of Old Barcelona, of carts pulled by ostriches?
Did I quote then that Arabic proverb, or
        say, *We'd ride their wings across firey bridges?*

The Moor
—for M

Let me be the Moor. You're the Galician Princess,
slavegirl. OK? I'm on my own Reconquista;
you're down on your knees. Yes,
I am an African who reads a lot,
and you are tilting back your wondrous head,
your dark hair twisted tight in my fist.
You are parting your balmed lips,
tongue taunting, bright as a bitten strawberry.
Yes, this is almost communion…
Are you on your hands and knees?
We're both slaves to the blur of the mirror.
Or do you want to be that famous pulpo gallego,
squiggling away in my inky mouth?
I am the Moor, and you, my almost conquered,
interrupt: *Enough History! Fóllame!*

Ghazal

Between us she is Latin, a dark metaphor
unutterable, open and pulsating: not fear.

We are holding her, fully, in this happiness, waking,
finding everything silences us, our tongues, eyes and her.

Now where is a kiss, where begins the licking, the violence
that as our hands tumble over—holding her in her fear?

Yes, my beloved, she is the One Between, deep as an ear,
and as you tongue at her dangling lobe I grasp her. Hear?

Darling, my Sweetness, are you really whispering, that incendiary,
angry? Are you hitting her in this dream? Am I holding her?

This is our pleasure… Are you slapping, whipping our Latina?
She is crying. Then you are crying, still, trembling with fear.

João

Idanha-a-Velha

Midst the cork groves,
"crows'-nests" high up the unrigged masts
imaginary fleets have abandoned
to daylight. Where are the lookouts
beholding an approaching shore?

In Idanha-a-Velha, the messy stork's nest,
like tumbleweed lodged atop the squat steeple
was a blank speech-bubble awaiting
this tale told by Juan Goytisolo in Dejemaa el-Fna,
then retold by a Magrabi poet:

> *The man from Marrakesh became a stork,*
> *flew across the Mediterranean*
> *seeking his wife who journeyed there to work.*
> *He found her in France, living with a businessman…*

With my distant Beloved in mind,
I am recalling this as I, heading back
towards the Spanish border, speed past another empty
stork's nest hovering on a tall plinth,
awaiting its hero.

Alicante

Nobody believes me when I say this city
looks like Waikiki, the beaches curving away
under their wall of new hotels and
on the lone bare mountain, where a cryptic
Diamond Head should be, the Moorish hallucination
of a Roman castle. They should: not far
away Wild West towns await a cinematic eye
and south, across the azure Mediterranean,
my doppelgänger stands in a striped galabia,
feet planted on the earth of Djemaa el-Fna,
and, with fado in his heart, he recites
into the ear of an old Goytisolo,
his poem on the lost Caliphate
and on the World-to-Come.

Cide Hamete Benengeli
—*The True Author of Don Quixote of La Mancha, on His Eternal Captivity*

"Camões lost his eye,
and Cervantes his hand.
My Soul was stolen
by a slaver, *John
Someone*: the White African."

Graffiti, Lavapies

Eu deberia ter mellorada miña sinatura.

Alfama

(No, remembering that poem
erased, 'lost', the only remaining
line on the razing of Casa da India
by the Lisbon Earthquake,
the evaporation of Australia
under an Islamic curse,

won't lead you to Chafiz do Dentro,
that font in the Old Muslim
Quarter where you'd like to wait
for the proverbial maiden, her
visitation, just as you had
in your refused future,
at the spring of the Old Brewery Site.

In this once pillaged city,
you are, at least, lost in the still-standing Moorish lanes
remembering one of your abandoned poems,
a last line:

And then there was Candide passing through…)

The Language

(to be translated into Farsi)

I will learn what the world is,
not from the beginning, that's
the impossibility of meaning,
but from that place where
shiny thoughts are twilight
and everything, like a child's first NO,
furthers the sun.

Like when I spoke with her today,
I will be naked, clear
and mute. (The rain falls
through me. The flowers unfold
as if they were afraid of my cold, sluggish
face that says:

Without her I would be broken…)

Hold on, I almost remember:

When she was THE SAME, the other woman, her sister…

To me we are the Same, just
as I must be this sameness in
my skin's noise and between all the leaves
of the books through whom I speak
whenever I hear other storms, small
animals and white language.

Her name is another woman's.

Her face, my heaven.

Her skin, God.

(I inscribe this inside myself.)

The woman here beside me
doesn't understand. Nor do I.

With me she sleeps
as though the world were intimate and curious.

Like a small animal, her tongue walks
around my face.

And when her tongue is over my eyes,
I remember the visionary,

and how he kissed his girlfriend:
her eyelids were translucent, stainless,

a flickering name…

*When, darkly, they were inside each other,
what did she see?*

A small cloud, cold and blue?

A name that, fleshed, could speak of the All?

*The exceptional silence they felt across the darkness,
stones?*

In other languages the song
of love, hope and death is
more serious, sinister, something

that in a bird's flight is only
a flash, a convincing
abstraction that eventually, quiet as waves,

explodes.

Azanians

The Auteur
—for João César Monteiro

Never an auteur, though sometimes 'a João',
of God, His Eye.

Yet—*A confession!*—on my deathbed,
my last sentence will, probably, begin,

"I…"

When He Suggested She Should Have Read the Story in a More Natural Voice—

"No utterance of the daemonic is unnatural."

Self-Portrait As a Camel Conjured by Daemons,
—a Persian carpet not in the Museu Gulbenkian

I'm afraid, a camel, luminous,
loping panicked away from the voice
asking: *Your monster?*
Me? Or that grinning demon
who leapt up on my hump,
who is twisting a malnourished snake
into a halter? Suddenly around me
the trees are a cage, pomegranates
pocked moons, faces zoological or bestial,
voices, that cacophony.

Question for António Damásio

Doesn't all European thought
disappear into the Void
between Spinoza and Pessoa,
that cornucopia
of nerves and that Tibetan
skull-cup?

Ghosts

I wondered
whether, like my translator,
the 'Angolana',
who was, without
having ever been
there, a colonial,
an accomplice,
whether I might
have been dead
pale, the chameleon
who, in a Malagasy
proverb, is un-
mirrored, phantasmagoric:

Ghosts are forever, until the magic is done.

Corpus

(Another poet tells me,
in his third language,
that Helder constantly refines his poems,
each edition of The Works
becoming shorter, a sea
eroding the shore.)

Imagine the ideal:
open water, a world all ocean.

What Should, Perhaps, Be Corrected

The only voice to whom I'm open
is that—GHOST—between
the Spoken.

Africans

There, in the village agora,
his speech is shimmering ocean waves,
clapping hands of afternoon light,
homely drumming,
and I am understanding
what he's singing,
though can't translate,
as though his words
could be my own thoughts,
as if this African in my Lisbon
dream were the real me,
and I, in overhearing us now,
am an angel.

Her Experience

Back from some work in Sydney,
my Mozambican-born friend was agitated.

While we luncheoned
in my dream of a Lisbon restaurant,

she explained that at a party
she had been attacked

for being South African.
As we ate she kept repeating,

"How can you live there
when they hate us so much?"

Fathers

The Australian ghost
who repeatedly writes
his life as a novel
claims as his father
the opium-addicted,
Chinese art-collecting
Symbolist of Macau,
Camilio Pessanha.
I recognize both
Australasian spectres
as my lost brothers,
though, in the poem
of my existence,
or 'disappearance',
let my absentee father
be registered as one
Solomon Mandela.

La Nacão

Condemned to antipodean exile
I may never master the mother-tongue of Spinoza

I, "Gentile", as my grandmother
the Jewess would call me,

who worried I wasn't baptized,
I, João de Deus,
the Headless…

O Lord, honey my tongue with Portuguese!
O Father, in my name, please sound the shafir!

Virgem do Leite
—a sculpture by João Alfonso, 1469

Unabstract as the Queen of Heaven
breast-feeding God's son,

her pitying, almost downcast eyes
seeing through abundance

to the Inquisition that would have figured
her as the First Image

had those men not been afraid
of their omnivorous Mother.

The Drowning of Bahadar Shah
—a miniature painting by La'l, circa 1603-4

Must be the Gujarati Sultan, that man
with his arms raised, sombre face—tiny
eyes!—turned towards us just above
the water, hoary and grey and swirling, that Indian Ocean
in which he's drowning, thought murdered,
surrounded by the other friendly heads floating like fruit
and the thudding boats manned by the busy Portuguese,
their black hats and pale hands pointing there and there
and there towards him.

Clamber up onto one of the boats, dear Sultan,
and prove us wrong! Return, triumphant, from the Invisible!

Ekphrasis

These Mozambican figures
in the billionaire's African Collection,
phantasmagoric. One of a spirit
standing on a man's bent back
and hacking into his spine, though the grimace
such he could have been eating flesh,
drinking from a skull-cup. Like the protean
in Mia Couto's tales: war's phenomenology,
how photos 'capture' what we either struggle
to remember or can't forget, our regressing
to the scene of the crime
as to a lost country, edenic.

The Hotel

Ahead of him, ascending the wooden stairs,
showing him the hotel, his room, ironically
remarking, in her secretive accent, slowly,
that for some reason she can't understand
why tourists like Oporto. In her maid's uniform
she is Fancy. He knew the hotel already
from his Melbourne dream, that sad night
when, envisioning himself arriving back in Portugal
by ship, disembarking to enter a rainy promise,
he'd fallen asleep listening to Madredeus:
O Teresa Salgueiro! Sweet Angel of Fado!
She, the maid, was the woman he might have loved
were the world not cynical, his dissociation
cliché. Her skirt shimmied up the back of her knees.
No music that night, only, in the next room,
coquettish and noisily kissing, an American tourist
with a local man she'd met earlier in the evening.
The poet had to admit that he wasn't Ricardo Reis,
hadn't returned from Brazil, wasn't worth a novel,
and knew: *Loneliness is only one's own absence.*

Sunday Night Tango at Teatro A Barraca

One of the nuances
of the dance: her leg
curling quickly around
his in an arabesque
of stiletto, quick
as the blade, then stilled
in mimic-fear. Eve
and Adam cheek-to-cheek
in the first move
of Mediterranean greeting,
this notional embrace.
So many truths revealed
in South American brothels!

Pessanha's House

Carlos, in his long black coat,
stands at the end of the bar
like a magi, listing the names
of cities in Africa and Asia,
giving his opinion on each.
Ana Paula, historian and poet,
with her big green maternal eyes,
listens, her Luanda of last week
vast as the Forbidden City.
And Mónica, too, my Galician love,
has in her heart, at very least,
Torre de Hércules. While Miguel,
the publisher, paces back and forth,
planning, plotting… The first
time I met Carlos was in Macau,
outside the smoky Á-Mà Temple,
he wore a black suit and walked us
along the Inner Harbour to show
the Wall of Dissimulation,
Pessanha's other home. In his essay
on the poet's house, it's a chaotic museum;
Chinese scrolls, statues, plates
everywhere, except in the bedroom
where Camilo sits, tearfully presenting
his mother's rosary. Carlos may be
right: there are the starry conurbations
of the departing world, and then,
always, the kindly void of the Mother.
Like this bar that, he says, he's
frequented over the decades,
each time under a different name.

Homage

Near the Sé, though below,
deep as the exhumed colosseum
dedicated to Nero,

this, the birthplace of Santo Antonio,
this crypt where his Image
—a child perched on Life's open book,

or on his arm like a stout parrot,
is peaceful, yellow—is a Jizō,
my Saint of the Homeless and the Lost.

I, kneeling, head bowed,
am the Unborn, unrecalled, an aborted echo.

Coimbra

Slitting open the pages of an edition
of *The Tragedy of Inês de Castro*,
reflecting on the experimental
poets of Coimbra, their insistence
on the dissolution of the FIRST PERSON,
you remember, earlier in the day,
picking oranges for the first time
in your life, floating, a cosmonaut,
between the suns in an Australian's
poem, and then, somehow anticipating Inês,
THE FIGURE, you must have read elsewhere,
as effigy, as corpse, you are wondering
whether your own dissolution has begun,
whether, between these memories,
you were SELF, or could be 'mere'
allusion, a cloud, drifting;

Poesia Incompleta

The Square

There, at the corner of Rossio,
between Teatro Dona Maria and São Domingos,
leaning against the railings, chatting, standing,
like messengers arriving too late or being too forgetful,
the Africans—*Do they know?*—are guarding
the spirit of an inconspicuous stone monument
to those condemned by the Inquisition.
I'd thought to see my Self among them,
waiting to present a polemic or, at least, recall
a poem. I saw, instead, the faces
of haunted men in a photo by Santu Mofokeng.
Then, in her patent-leather shoes and summer-blue dress,
my sweetheart was there awaiting
me—*my Soul*—with a smile
greater, kinder than any memory.

The Bookshop

There in the back room of Poesia Incompleta
—*What a wonderful name!*—my beloved
and I could have fucked out of the joy
of Literature. (Porno title: *Corto Maltese and his Muse*;
script by J Matteo.) Of course we didn't,
not with our friend on the sofa in the front of the shop,
smoking cigarillos and reading. Especially not in this city
where baroque syntax and a luminous noun
are the shortest route through the alleys and one-way streets up
and up to the secluded miradouro of my half-heartedly
foreign Soul.

Fado
—after J Slauerhoff

Am I ruined because I'm sad,
finding all futile and corrupt,
feeling my only need's
the shade of an umbrella?

Or am I sad because I'm ruined,
never to enter the world,
only to know Lisbon from the Tejo,
to be here a Nobody?

Instead, I wander through the dark
impoverished lanes of Mouraria,
encountering many who, like me,
are bereft of love, desire and hope…

Poet Without Qualities

His wagon is homemade,
the kind only pulled by the Will.
The tiny dog on that assemblage
barks half-musically, comically.

The man, a statue up there, sings
or shouts through a cardboard cone,
warning the people of the Baixa
of our impending doom and drama.

From the balcony of my pensão
I listen to him, that promoter of Visions.
He looks painted by Grão Vasco.
His name must be unambiguous: *João*.

Documents

Somewhere in the dossier
on his talk at Centro de Estudos
Camonianos, was that reference
to his Being's marginalia,
that twice naming of things
in Macao, of the streets
and that bottle of wine:
SEM AMEGIOS.
The irony of Elsewhere.

This Era

  Philosophical as always,
the Indonesian poet's essay
   on the Indian Ocean Tsunami
as the Lisbon Earthquake of our day,

   questions, not quite as Voltaire did,
the Future that always follows disaster,
   that wakefulness
after each, *Inshallah!*

"My House Is Empty"

Everyone wants
to own things, others,
land. Me?
It's too late.
My house is empty.
You don't believe
me? Come inside
my hacienda.
See: *Kosong*!
Furnished only
by my Iranian
friend's dream.
She saw
my house
inside painted
white by a man
humming an Arabic
song.

An Aquaintance

"Promise not to write about me."

Late into the night she reads Musil in the original
and remembers, fitfully, when life wasn't a surveillance balloon
black and drifting over another century.

Os Elefantes Brancos

The Ex-Photographer

        Strange for the Poet to meet him here,
in the Capital of the Anglophone Empire,
R, this ex-Photographer who had been
in the townships during the Emergency
and in Mozambique during the war, where
he learnt his Portuguese. Here
they're in a jungle, almost lost in the Ecology
of Everyone. That's Capital, isn't it – the Rome
of Apuleius the Magi, worshipper of Isis, or
the later world of Saint Augustine,
that other African? They order dinner
from a Sri Lankan lady who still wears
her sari under the anorak. A selection
of curries on the plate and the Poet has
a flash-back to sitting alone in a tourist restaurant
not far from the conflict-zone in her country
a few months before, having travelled
along roads where a soldier was posted every
five hundred meters, and where, at the ancient Buddhist
cities, beggars appeared in the dusty parking lots,
mothers toting their children,
and he'd gone from one defunct site
of the Buddha's Tooth Temple to another,
asking the guide why the Tooth was Sovereign,
why there had been wars over the relic.
The guide had surmised that every time
the Dharma was uttered those words
streamed past and purified the Tooth. The Buddha's
Tooth as Stupa circumambulated by
the Teachings. These Azanians, the Poet
and the ex-Photographer, have their own: Refuge
in Lisbon—where they had been
introduced—with Mandela as their Buddha,
and their Dharma, or the beginnings of,

in The Struggle. "You know," R says,
"It's really strange to be here. The last time I
was here was to lecture at Goldsmiths. I saw
my name the other day, as 'Visiting
Professor'. Now I'm a student
working on software for Cape Verdean children!"
He's been back and forth to Boston,
Cape Verde, returning home to Cape Town;
his wife and children stay in Lisbon.
The Poet is remembering a pasta dinner with them
in their apartment there, their conversation
about the visit the previous week
of a now famous photographer,
and in his mind he'd seen one
of his Works: a man, a cane-cutter, who in
digital vividness was a rural chic,
that illusion. (Later in the evening
the police had arrived to talk
with R's wife. She'd lodged a complaint
that the girls of Elefante Branco, the club
across the road, were having 'liaisons'
in their apartment building. R had said
that one day at a cafe or park, his wife
had met one of those girls,
and the young Brazilian had explained
that she didn't want to be working
there, that it was a notorious place, infamous
in the Portuguese World, even among
mining engineers in Angola, and her mother
back in Brazil had explicitly
asked her to not end up there.)
The Poet asks R if he ever missed
been a photographer. "Not at all.
It was a weapon in the Struggle. The other
day I came across a book, a book
with my photos. It was from those days, those
crazy times, when I was working hard,

drinking and sleeping rough.
I got to know Kylesha, was
interested in the hostel-dwellers. Once
you're known in a place like
that, and the right people think you're ok,
you can really see things. So I started documenting
the people living there. It was a whole world,
that hostel, with its own politics based
around the bed. Each bed was
a house, everything circled around
that. It's strange for me to now see that work
called 'illustration', and the difference
between the various editions: On the cover
of the SA book my name is there
with the author's. On the American it's not.
Sometimes you can think these things happen
because you're White…" The Poet's story
is different: two immigrations, a life of
what used to be called 'inner-exile'. He
tells R that his father kept them moving,
his father couldn't make up his
mind where they should live. His father's
last days were spent in Jo'berg after
all. R says, "It's hard to remember
what those days were like now. You can forget
that Apartheid, something so important
in your life, might mean nothing
to other people. A while ago I was
looking at YouTube and I thought I'd
show my son some videos of Mandela, teach
him something about our history. It's
amazing what you find there! I showed
him the speech from the day of the Release, the video
of him leaving the gates of the prison. You
know, when I was running the museum
on Robben Island he met Madiba?
But you know what really impressed him? Not

all of that or the stories we'd told
him, but when he saw the footage
of the FREE MANDELA concert. Yes!
He said to me, "Gees Dad, that old man
was so famous Wembley Stadium was full of people
wanting him to go free!" He knows
how big Wembley Stadium is: we
watch a lot of soccer." He laughs and keeps eating,
like an African, a peasant, until his plate
is clean. To the Poet, the memory
of Mandela's release is of waiting
with his family in front of the TV in their dingy
house in suburban Perth, waiting to see
that man's face—he'd only ever seen one picture
of the Legend—to see how he had aged, how noble
he might be, and with his parents wondering
why it had all happened just after they'd
left. The Great Man's image, banned
for almost three decades. R: "The thing
about that, having worked all those years as a photographer,
fighting Apartheid with pictures of what was
really going on, is that I didn't see that
moment, the moment when he slowly walked
out of the prison gates. I was
in Mozambique. The war was still going
on. I didn't see the first pictures for
a while afterwards because the newspaper
in Maputo couldn't afford to buy
any syndicated ones. They went
through their files and all they could find was that image
of him as a boxer. You know that famous
one? Well, that's what was on the front page
of the newspaper in Maputo on the day
he was released. The Judge Albie Sachs
tells the story of how, in those days
during the war, the Mozambicans
were running out of supplies and they

had to choose between making paper for toilet-paper
or newspaper. And they chose newspaper! Actually,
I think it's just one of his parables. So
I never saw those pictures that everyone else did
till I got back to SA. I remember
sitting in a shack in the shantytown
outside Maputo and listening with a stack
of other people to the event being described on
a little tinny radio." The Poet remembers
having memorized the Moment of Emancipation
in a poem: Mandela as a flame, as
the Personification of Justice, as Moses
entering the Promised Land. Though for him
and his family it was no longer the promised
land: they were on their way to
becoming Australian. And he thinks
back to those speeches by Bishop Tutu he'd heard
over the years, on the People in Captivity,
of the Flight from Egypt. Everything
changed on seeing Madiba walk
out into the Glorious Day. Then he's thinking
back to that Lisbon night when he'd had dinner
with R and his family, breaking bread with
them, his own experience of Issac Singer's story,
where the Writer, visiting the White City, a city
built on seven hills, like Jerusalem,
like Rome, like Macau or Rio,
and the Writer's constantly reflecting
on the Jews, their plural Exodus. Accumulating
details of their lives, their presence, the tale
ends with him having dinner with a family
who, through their Judaic resemblance
—Was it a Sabat meal?—makes him feel
he's in an Eternal past. But when the Poet
had left the family's apartment, going down
the dimly lit stairwell, passing the two hostesses
from Elephante Banco who were leading

a tipsy middle-aged man up to
their studio, he'd had a guilty
moment when he longed to be that man,
one who could lose himself in imageless
bliss among the illusion of Others.

The Translator

          Whenever the Poet thinks of the Translator,
he thinks of that café on Praça Figueira,
and of looking across to see an African
talking with his friend. Not talking,
just listening, smiling with an unearthly contentedness,
angelic. And the Poet had tried to think of when he
had ever seen an European that happy.
The Translator, L, had been introduced to him
by a Johannesburg anthologist, someone
he would later imagine might have been L's lover
or at least part of the same Scene. L had spoken
about the past, the Struggle, activism, what his left-wing
credentials had been, and how—he only half
explained—he couldn't return to SA.
He had been in Lisbon for years, teaching English
to children and Literature, via the Web, to US marines
in Iraq and Saudi Arabia. His East Rand accent, a voice
from one of the Poet's previous lives. The Poet
had found himself speaking of the possibilities
he had lost: not knowing a Nguni tongue, being a nobody
even among the ghostly Australians.
"Times change, hey," the Translator had said, discoursing
then on his other lives, as a union organizer, of befriending
Indians and Coloureds, learning
about their lives, realizing that he must join
in to fight Apartheid. (A year later
L would visit the Poet and his Muse in their Alfama
apartment, reminisce on the clarity of Highveld air,
the smell and yellow of the minedumps where
as a child he'd played. And the Muse would turn
to ask the Poet: *Did you also have that life?*)
That first day, the Translator had suggested a walk, up
the sloping mosaic pavement of Avernida Liberdade,
and as they walked, he talked about Coetzee

and Gordimer, their feud, his memory of a lecture
Coetzee had given in Cape Town when, scared off
by a bomb-threat, Rushdie had cancelled; it was the time
of the fatwa. She had invited Coetzee
to replace him. "All she had wanted to speak
about was Freedom of Speech, her idea of it,
to defend it. Coetzee made her furious. He'd been reluctant,
suggesting that maybe it wasn't universal, that maybe
we need to think carefully about whether we should
criticize a Sacred Book. I don't know if she ever spoke
to him again! Anyway, she hates everyone called 'John'…"
Just as well I've never met her, the Poet'd thought.
And as they walked, striding, not the Poet's usual ambling,
L explained that he had been working on a critical biography
of Gordimer based on reading her fiction biographically.
"A problem?" the Poet had suggested. The Translator, undaunted,
had replied he knew enough about her and had done
all the necessary critical and psycho-analytical reading.
His problem was the boredom; he had already written
500 pages. The image of Gordimer and Coetzee on a stage
under the banner of Freedom of Speech while the world
outside was crazed, cars upturned as roadblocks,
buses burning, schools looted, the boy-soldiers in brown vehicles
wondering which smoky country they were in
while children pelted them with rocks, wondering whether
they were a thousand Jonah's inside hippos
swimming through rivers of smoke… The Anthology
that had initially brought the Poet to Portugal,
had included Camões as the first European poet
of Africa, and Pessoa as a Durbanite. There was Rui Knopfli's
poem, too, an ode to iGoli that ends with a boy, a shepherd,
in the street, playing on his pennywhistle "a kwela
for tomorrow." That joyful cliché! Why not—weren't
the Great Schitzoid Pessoa's own last words,
in English: "I will see what tomorrow will bring"?
The aubade of a clerk! And as they'd walked back to the Baixa
from Marquês de Pombal, the Poet realized they were passing

the apartment of a friend and the notorious Elefante Branco,
and L had asked: "Oz. Are you happy there?" As always,
the Poet had given the descriptions of the Dutch explorers,
that New Holland was flat and barren, full of marvels,
like cockatoos and kangaroos, and the warm ashes of campfires
abandoned by hiding Aboriginal folks. As usual,
he had spoken of the logic of the penal, the dreams
of Currency Lads and Lasses, and of his poem on Yagan,
of that silence under the skin like a glass splinter
impossible to remove. Like his other European friends,
L had asked him why he's still there, and the Poet had answered:
"I am riding on the shoulders of my Soul,
unable to direct my path by thinking. Often
he has a mind of his own, wades across the River Styx,
while I am up there imagining it's the shimmering Tejo,
or the black waters of the Swan…" The Translator
had shaken his head, clear he would never go there.
Another Azanian friend said worse, that the place
must be dokum, cursed, and the Poet'd had to agree.
When they strode'd along the Tejo—they had been
walking the entire afternoon—L spoke of the Mozambican,
Eduardo White, a poet in a suit and dark glasses
who'd had to give his recent reading with his face
bandaged: "The night before he'd got into a fight
with some Cape Verdeans. Over a woman, of course!
And it was in a Cape Verdean restaurant…" (M, the Poet's
Lisbon publisher, had told him about White a few nights
before, in almost an allegory: "He only became a poet
because he had a government post he didn't want.
He was in the Agricultural Ministry. In those days
the Communist government nominated you for a position,
and it was final. It was possible to leave the post
if you had a good reason. His friend said that he should join
the Writers' Union. If you were a member of the Union
you could get a salary and some kind of status.
But you needed to have published a book. White resigned
and wanted to register as a Writer, although he didn't have a book.

And he was close to getting into serious trouble
with the Party. The Day of Reckoning was getting close,
and still he hadn't written anything. He hadn't written
anything before. So White decided
he needed to isolate himself. He took a bottle of wine
and went up to his friend's balcony over-looking the Indian Ocean,
vowed he wouldn't leave until he had written
the book. That's how he wrote his first book.
He's a genius. Mozambique's Rimbaud!")
The Translator had little time for him,
just another poet in his Anthology that would appear
in London during Black History Week.
Then they'd gone to Amazéns in Chaido, to the top floor
of the mall. In the imitation Brasileira, the Poet
looking out over the city towards a sun-gilded Castelo
Saõ Jorge, keeping his gaze there, had asked
what L had against Gordimer to merit
reading her stories against her life. "Something serious,"
he'd said. "Something very bad." He wouldn't say more,
and the Poet hadn't asked more, hadn't want to know.
L spoke a bit more, alluding to secrets, a suicide.
The Poet inferred other things, too, and suddenly
the danger of their South African past had been rediscovered,
in a moment they were hijacked by who they were,
by who others thought they were. That's War: *Everyone
is Other*. Rimbaud's dream. Maybe that's why it wasn't strange
for Rimbaud to become an arms-dealer and slaver?
Less strange than L's telling the Poet's girlfriend,
at their future dinner in Alfama, that one day
he woke, having heard a loud bang—he was living
in a hostel in downtown Jo'burg—and he'd gone outside
to find that the building next door had been blown up.
The Muse would look at her love horrified, her eyes asking,
Is this true? What kind of a country are you coming from?
L would then also tell the Poet, though in New York
an Afrikaans poet already had, of what had happened to Coetzee;
that Mbeki had written an unsigned communiqué

labelling *Disgrace* an example of the Unreconstructed
Whites. L would laugh: "Presidents are literary
critics, too, you know!" It was shortly after that 'incident'
that Coetzee left for Adelaide, an exile even for Australians,
where he became a citizen, took the Oath
of Allegiance in front of a specially invited audience
in a tent at the Writers' Festival. "In the newspaper
he was even in an advert for people to take out
citizenship," the Poet would say. "I think I was the only person
to read the sad, elusive and exclusive interview
he gave to *The Bulletin* on his arrival." "Why do you
think that?" "Because it hit the streets
on a date that's easy to remember:
September 11, 2001." But then, later on that first day,
a day as long as Joyce's *Ulysses,* the Poet
had stood outside the door of his pensaõ
to bid L farewell and found himself describing the Double
Voice of the Poem. L had told the Poet that he had originally
been a Novelist and in those days was involved with COSAW,
what had been an answer to PEN. Gordimer had made
him Treasurer. And when he'd been working
on one of his novels, he'd suddenly realized
that the character was based on her, and that another
was, too, and that he had actually been writing about her,
engaging in a long argument with her.
That was when he became interested in her psychology,
the kind of person she'd made herself into: "This
tough ambitious Bitch from the East Rand, My World,
who had charmed herself into a Grand Dame of Letters!"
For a moment, the Poet had seen her standing behind L,
Hydra-headed. Then he'd seen the Translator—or her?—in
a Hall of Mirrors, turning and turning to find the Other. Yes,
Lisbon is not a city of a Rimbaud, but of that proliferating ghost,
Fernando Pessoa, the First Person.

Monsanto

You are still dreaming
> when from the rock ledge over which you might tumble,
> vertiginous and free, you
see into the next dream,
> a starlit mirror, Pleiades flying like salt over your shoulder,
> you the silhouette that sparkling
is sparked by,
> and in looking down
into the mountains crumpling into each other's quiet
> you must be seeing the infinity
from which you might never escape unless you wake now.

The mountain as dice-thrower.
One toss: a crown of boulders.
Another: a castle.

    Who is there to read the dice?
    Who to win or lose?

Up here among the winds,
        the Human begins by placing one rock
against another.
        A home might be accretions of stones
around a huge round boulder
        that would be the roof, sky solidified.

The Human begins with the simplest question,
        despite doubting whether in this dream
you're on a mountain
or on an island.

Enter another stone house,
its ossuary.

(Were the world created
anew, daily,

you would leave there
'as old as could be'.)

Over the valley, its village,
its nearby mountain like broa
gnawed by famished children,

the house is a staring face
behind which you, all-seeing,
an homunculus, can't exist.

There, in the valley,
you 'catch a glimpse'
of a poupa, far away,
as he alights
then disappears, and you
remember, maybe dreaming,
an Unseeing from
your previous life.
Neither spoke, yet you heard
this: *I am the Messenger
of the Invisible. I know
the Way…* And you still
try to follow.

Roof, lime-lichened tiles and rotten beams, caving-in,
then the walls, maybe, though they decompose like music,
collapsing fast, or one solid phrase
at a time, rock from there,
here, bright moss soundproofing its shifting placement.

    Then, in an archaeological mood,
you, Wandering Stranger, register a rubble of remembered stones
on the roadside veld deep in your colonial childhood
as silence:

Neolithic, an unsettlement.

You are told that the women of the village,
on festival day, will carry their faceless dolls
up to the castle for the view, and join in flinging down
the terracotta pot of Spring flowers
at the enemy who left centuries ago.

Descending from the windy
bouldered path and its castro, you
are an eye, omni-hopeful,
a glass eyeball rolling,
bouncing, clicking like an African's
tongue, down from the earliest
inhabitation, its ghosting,
down, down through the stone
streets, past stone houses
and larger stone houses,
walls, moss-cloaked granite,
every stone, every wall a presence,
every presence a wall, until
the largo of the next village
and you keep bounding,
skittish, roaming, the falling eye
of an unbroken God.

Am I hearing a mbira warmed up by twenty thumbs?

No, it's the flock of sheep down there in the misty valley.

Two russet haired goats,
> with typical self-assurance,
whether thanks to horns or,
> as a Triestene once described,
their 'Semitic' faces.
> They remain among the sheep
who in their weathered flock,
> individuated by names and bells,
graze contentedly, sheepishly.
> They all have mind enough to
stop and stare up at you,
> passing Stranger.

You are not dreaming that you are led through a village
where not a century ago the peasants were barefoot slaves

living in windowless stone houses and from their 'Brazilian' palace
the landed kept them and their ancient church in ruins.

Nor are you dreaming that the baby held and kissed repeatedly
by her grandmother is the only child in the village.

You aren't dreaming that she is watching you with a judiciousness,
with the large dark eyes, of a recently woken Baby Jesus.

The young women's faces painted white,
they stand lining the street
that slips away like a breeze,
wait like the spirits of blossoming trees.
You walk among them, through
their clouds, talking wordlessly with your Love,
'making eyes', playing at being strangers,
and the church bells are ringing, adufes
trembling, ticklish under village women's fingers.

There is the singing heard only by you…

Where, the other night, that woman waited
alongside the stone road, you find,
descending the road with your Beloved—You're
never ascending!—closing your eyes,
you have almost passed her,
that old woman who throws up her arms,
casting a white bedsheet over you both,
and you are flooded with blindness,
bright warmth, are blessed.

      In the next dream
that Galician witch again throwing up her arms,
casting confetti over you both,
and you wake, telling your Love—

Two bell-towers,
both 'clocked'.

Between each
pealing of their hour

a few minutes'
discrepancy that

you allow to be
infinite, or

Monsanto.

Stones: if you would eat
them, you would be stronger
than this blindness. Day,
above the village, below the ruined
castle, on the lichened rock-lip
about to utter the valley,
is sporadic in the thin grass,
and night is this stone rondavel
roofed with earth that
in Spring is a small disc
of flowering meadow. Stones:
in your dreams you eat
them, everywhere. You eat the castle,
the village, the whole bright world.
You, Black Pig, who,
cannibalized, will feed them
through the Winter, they
who eat your body, drink
your blood, they who, when
with a long iron spike gather
round to pierce your heart
and stare into your eyes
to watch their blurry selves
and block their ears
against your screaming that's
this blind world
dying in giving birth
to more stones.

Around the boulder
        their home of ordered rubble,
almost invisible.

        Invited in, you find
the boulder's
        a wall, close,

bulging with the Invisible.

Then, there was your Beloved
on her haunches, knees spread,

leaning back on a mossy rock,
naked, her pale skin blinkingly

bright, hiding more than one
sun. She was the Holy Virgin

who dreams of a sweet New World
Maria to tease and slap and fuck

in your presence, Mountain God.

An impregnable keep…

      Those words you remember,
eventually, the next day,
      after the dream. Which

dream? There were two.
      Those words of a Lyrik
returning to you, like a breeze,

as you walk the ruined castle wall,
words rock-clear;
      like that cynical, upsetting dream

from which you woke
      shocked, you, that tormented terracotta
pot full of flowers

toppling from the castle wall.

("Did you
visit yet,"
the student
asks again,
"the University
Prison?" You
meant to.
You hear
yourself
again, not
saying you
couldn't,
not that cave,
under the Baroque
library, where
the students
were taken
during the Salazar
years.)

Undreamt.

She remembers, decades before,
being a child at the village wedding,
the iron bowl and spoon,

staring down into her reflection
between the smashed potato boulders,

your face,

down there in the thick mirror
of pig's blood.

(Twelve Poems)

Homage to Avraham Ben Yitzhak

Between the Name of the Patriarch
and of his Son, the Poet

is silent, an intervening Angel.

Somebody tells me
the only Person who spoke the Lord's

Name was the Mother
of the Poet's Double.

Did the Poet and the Father
build the Kaa'bah?

Or did their Doubles?

I thought God had Ninety-Nine Names?

The Unpronounceable: *To not create the First Person.*

Yet to build a Second House…

Later, a Descendent of the Double
would return to the Festival of Poetry

to empty the House of Images,
make an Image of Emptiness.

Where in the argument are 'The Satanic Verses'?

Then, centuries later, in Vienna's Café-Museum,
the Names of the Son and the Patriarch

wouldn't be enough to return
the Poet to Being;

his Father passed away,
his Mother's home razed,

his lost writings had been replaced
by twelve anonymous poems.

Let his Name be Unwritten, as he wished.

*Let his Silence be an echo
of these, his words:*

"On seven roads we depart and on one we return."

Meydan

'Medan'

What remains artefact,
passed over
by looters—

not the thing
exchanged;

a word loaned
is inviolable, a meeting
place, or

a battlefield.

The Aryan Face of Nefertiti
—*after Martin Bernal*

Black, like the doorway
between the Mosque of the Soul
and the Pilgrims' Hostel
of the Face: Athena's

assumed visage, as the Ace
of Spades, no less there
than Nefertiti in her avatar,
Hitler's beloved statue.

They say, when the Ancients
painted a face black
they meant 'fertile'… An Afrikaner
poet once wrote: *Poets are born black,
whitening with age.*

The Copts

There, where two fingers
would find a pulse,

on the inside of his wrist,
he has the Coptic Cross

tattooed, a vital sign,
an amulet, almost secret,

like a word, Pharaonic,
surfacing to remain in Arabic,

a voice, calming, calling
across centuries of noise.

"We Are All Khalid Said"

No, that wasn't a knock
at the door that woke you.

Nor was that a skull
thudding, once, against a wall
on the floor above.

You'd fallen asleep
reading an article
about the man whose caved-in

face 'sparked' the Revolution,
his photo on a banner
held high in Midan Tahrir

when a million remembered
who they were:

        WE ARE HIM.

(On the next day's front-
page the deposed dictator's
eyes were half closed.)

While you, wide awake now,
are him:

WE ARE ALL SOMEONE
ELSE.

The Translator and the Poets

Hurghada

With an arabesque Sameer's open hand
drew the imaginary beard
of those, those who are ruining Alexandria,

accosting his daughter for not being veiled.
Afrophile and moustached, his glasses
twin-coins quietening his face. His pride,

he explained, was in having translated Gordimer.
When at the Cairo Book Fair, wordlessly
presenting a copy to her for a signature,

he recited the novel's first sentence as password.
Later, back at his family apartment,
the Koran-heavy block of his Arabic *The Famished Road*

was in my hands, while he, leaning forward from the couch,
watched on their old television a dull Tom and Jerry.

He muttered: "Much better this than those protestors,
the children and veiled women marching in Syria…"

Cairo

Mohamed, at the bar of the Cosmopolitan Hotel
used the word "martyrs" for those who
were killed during the Revolution. The American
professor, with whom I had been discussing Persian

Medieval poetry and Adonis' Sufi metaphors,
almost objected, wordlessly reminding our friend
that the Bearded Ones, too, might call them that.
We, Poets of Another World, ordered another beer.

I asked about Adonis. Mohamed and the others admire
the Poet, not the Spokesman. Recently, in an open letter
to the Syrian President, Adonis hadn't been denunciatory,
had been conciliatory, spoken carefully, like someone

afraid of evil. Ahmed, poet, once a prisoner, just listened.
In mind, the televised crowds of children and veiled women,
demonstrations sans men, were Voice yearning for utterance,
metaphor neither fundamentalist nor martyred.

Six Months After the Revolution
—at Maydan Tahrir

You watch one of those sandwiches drop from the tray on his shoulder. After contemplating what to do, this young pedlar of snacks at the Carnival of the Revolution surreptitiously puts it back. Then he wants to speak with you. He only knows how to say his name and ask if you speak Arabic. You know less, maybe only "Maydan Tahrir". You have already been asked for your passport by young men like him —students, unemployed?—who frisked you, then, friendly, patted your shoulder. You'd seen a stout woman in a burka who could have been his mother lamenting her deceased son with a declaration penned on a large Egyptian flag. Gazing away, cocking his head, sifting through his lexicon, he asks: "Your country?" You answer, are initially misunderstood. Then a man is speaking to him in Arabic. You ask the man what he said. "I was telling him to leave you alone." Then, despite himself, he is translating for the young man: "He is asking you for a dollar." You reach into your pocket. The man is speaking, fast. You feel mad for thinking he has all the acumen of an undercover policeman. "Don't give him any money," he says. Around the three of you, a small gathering of men, in broken English, apologize to you— only you— on behalf of Democracy, leaving the sandwich-seller and you to stalk away into dusk's growing crowd. There are loved-ones bearing placards, faux-Bedouin selling flags, young promenading couples, every kind of Egyptian, none of them knowing how this will end.

Winsor Hotel
—an Ur Poem

Gloaming is the room's
natural state. All the furniture
at least half a century old,
the lighting fluorescent tubes
that need to be tapped to glow
over the desk and the bed like
ectoplasms. Outside, Cairo
is a ruined cinema, piles
of rubbish and a row of orange
plastic chairs for the shisha
smoking men. I should join
them instead of being here
in another century, at the desk,
a hopefully novelist, or,
as I am, an ambiguous African
just woken from the dream
that I was giving refuge
to an Angolan warlord. I'm
more Tutuola's television-
handed ghost, gazing at my love
naked in a Hong Kong hotel
room. On the handset's screen,
there she is, blowing bubbles, clearly,
totally fuckable. Kowloon
somewhere outside, falling
away from the window.

> *(Remove the everyday from this,*
> *and the picture could be*
> *my qasida: The Lover returns*
> *to an abandoned campsite,*
> *recalling his Beloved, their "tryst"...)*

Cats of Zamalek

Universal are the cats
of Zamalek, 'at once',
as the English say, the kitten
toying with Mumbai rubbish, licking
the sauce off a take-away wrapper
and a mummified beast,
yellow eyes glinting emerald
at that nanosecond when we stumble
on Time. Universal these cats,
if miniature. Our presence
in passing is exaggerated,
colossal, sphinx-like
only in ruin.

Their Donkey

That donkey, three thousand years old,
if a day, has seen empires rise and fall,
has carried men, pulled wagons,
stood out in the barely bearable sun
while his owners have taken coffee
in shady cafes sucking on the shisha's tip
as on their mother's rubbery teat.
Their donkey, ragged, a discarded carpet,
on all fours, peaceful as a table,
waits, not wondering on the returning owners,
nor needing to glimpse a vacant face.
The donkey, remaining patient, yoked
to his weary but reliable vehicle
of a body, a real, if not metaphysical ambition,
retains his composure, his slave's aloofness,
and reminds himself that he was once employed
by the famous Joseph and Mary. As I said,
he was three thousand years old,
if a day.

On the Way to an Oasis,
a Traveller Reflects on His Fate

More than a decade ago I began this journeying.
In Java, at an embassy party, I met that fellow,
Second Secretary at the British Embassy,
an Etonian, friend of the Royal Family.
His girlfriend a newsreader on Indonesian tv.
Before introducing me, an acquaintance
had stated: "He has his eye on the Big Picture."
When we spoke, on writing, and I told of my book,
and of my wrestling with the Angel of Ambiguity,
that my habitation was the Pit of Silence,
he described his Papuan chronicles and plan
to walk around the globe. Immediately
in my mind's eye, he was Rhodes, colossal,
in that famous print of the Great Man mid-stride,
one boot on Cape Town, the other on Cairo,
measuring out the Dark Continent. Now his books
are reviewed in *The New York Times*.
After being Governor of two provinces in Iraq,
he's now an OBE and MP for Penrith and the Border.
Whereas I, my travelogue demolished by ex-colleagues,
am an occasional lecturer in a country that isn't mine
and have poems instead of memories, legend
in lieu of presence. I, Ozymandias,
Failed Travel-Writer…

Resident

Two tourists noticed the Russian woman before,
when she went into the Best Way Supermarket. Now
that they have had a better look at her
and at the man beside her holding her hand,
the one nudges the other: "That's what my friend
told me about. Russian women come here for sex
and to sell sex." The woman doesn't register
them. She's used to being noticed. Were she to explain
herself she would say: "Life is too difficult
in Moscow. Here in Hurghada, our Krasnomorsk,
I have work, a house, the sun and a man
who loves me. Yes, when I arrived I was a gogo-dancer,
an animator in hotels, a diving instructor. I
sell apartments now. My son and mother
are also here. In my purse, the Urfi certificate.
If I need to divorce I could tear it up,
easy. Why should I? He is my Pasha
and I am his Caucasian Queen."

The Nigerian Novelist

Asking our friend the Nigerian novelist
about Tutuola. She's indignant.

"You like that! They are just folk tales.
In my country we have seven hundred tongues.
In every one of them tales like that!
Folk tales! If we all write them down
the situation will be impossible!" Yet

she tells of lecturing to a thousand students,
of Yahoo Boys emailing out
pleas for financial help and their other fictions
and the Twin Dwarves of Nollywood,
that universe of cheap moralizing and Occult.

"All worse than folk tales!" she declaims,
then threatens to include us in her endless novel.

At Twilight

       After offering hashish
the taxi-driver, foot to the floor,
turns the Luxor pop

full-blast. The singing voice
megaphone metallic, a mirage,
we speed through,
an azan
wherein

we hover—

St Anthony's Cave

Balustrade. Top metal corner of a short staircase
that took you by the hand, down into the cave's
small dark. Of the space, your eyes
made, slowly, place enough for the imagined
Mass conducted pre-dawn by three monks
and for the altar on which the Saint's portrait
was propped, relaxed, against the rough wall.
Above, almost a vertical rock-pool for a toppling
narcissism, Christ's face aqueous behind glass.
The only illumination and air must be from the tunnel
back to the cliff. Your impulse is to lie where
the Saint would have, on one of those worn carpets,
to sleep like a vagrant. And while you drift there,
all those basements and crypts you have seen through the years
are one hazy gilded cave, a mineshaft down to the Soul.
Then your eyes close, and you aren't even there.

Valley of the Kings

Back there
in the Underworld,
under the cool
blatant rock
where we stared
up at the ceiling,
at Nut, Sky-
Goddess, snaking over
half the painted
world. She swallows
the bitter pill
of the roundest Sun,
nightly, as if
every morning
could be.

Ode

Ersatz palm-tree
taller than all
we see here
in the desert,
over the gated-
community. I realize
you are not
a minaret
broadcasting calls
to prayer: you
are a mobile-
phone tower,
pantheist in aspiration,
disguised, a flag
white and urging
us towards you.
In al-Rahman's
Iberian ode
to a palm-tree
you were personal,
a proud beacon,
fellow exile,
memory of Damascus,
the civilization
he was yearning
for. Whereas this,
my ode, is to you,
dear Friend, your
falsity and truth,
new tower
of Babel.

Red Sea

What she appeared as in the dream
can be said to seem more than hallucinatory:

a dilation of the Mind's Eye,
some body falling upwards into the sky

—That woman persistent in her burka,
standing there forever. *I don't know her.*

~

When in my dream I appear
I'm nothing like John Mateer.

I'm an old Chinese man with chopsticks fossicking
through dust, bones and ashen things

for a gold nugget, a radiance,
that will have him sing.

~

Where the pool is in the courtyard
of the hotel, there was an Ottoman garden,

an anti-Hell, oil-lamps under buttery tulips
and bright candles on my tortoise-shell.

There I was, Emissary of Slowness,
and of all this dream can't tell.

This Is Not a Land That Is Seen

It sees you.
It empties concrete dwellings,
bypasses checkpoints,
listens to Nothingness,
if it could be.

White rock,
calcified mountains,
sky too hot to be seen.
This is not desert.
It's a site cleared
for the Impossible.

There you are, Bedouin
of Mind, trying
to stand in your own
shadow.

~

Dusk wind: sandstorm,

a personless hate,
every confusion of sense:
hot fog, abrasive drizzle.

We emerge from the blown,
our lisping tongues
sandpaper—

"From dust to dust."

The Bridge

Yuhanna Al-Armani, the Coptic Painter

"Yuhanna," they will say, "was not our first master painter.
The others' icons were burnt, crushed for oil to anoint the living.
Besides, his art was of Jerusalem, and he, like Our Saviour,
was born there. Only Armenian in name, he was not a Copt,
not one of us, we descendants of the Pharaohs."
Not once would I respond to that. In my heart, Yerevan
was as white as Ararat, as Al-Azhar Mosque. That I, too, was Egyptian,
Cairene, meant less to me than those visions tethered to my signature.
Look at just one of my pictures—Gabriel, the Archangel,
the Annunciator. Always a popular choice for the reception rooms
of the recently rich… True, on occasion, I would exhibit
in the marketplace. Some said, "Thus his fame." Like my adoptive Copts,
I had pictures instead of words, Arabic gnawing my mother-tongue.
We were vagabonds in a Turkic Empire! Behold all my painted saints,
haggard prophets, hypnotic angels? They are only men,
wingéd, fugitive. The Holy Virgin and Child, too, merely refugees
fleeing into the desert, into Egypt. Can papers, signatures save us from that?
My comfort is my craft, in the spontaneity of Gift. While they believe
I emerged from Oblivion, clutching the Holy City's magic paint-brush,
all I actually ever painted were marginalia from illuminated Armenian Bibles,
even my own self-portrait.

On Galata Bridge

The Translator

Misty morning, my Love and I crossing Galata Bridge,
from the West to the East.
An infinity of fishermen leaning to retrieve their slivers of night.
And there's Marjan—translator of Milton,
Chaucer, *Beowolf.* Slovene poet!—collar up, smoking,
staring at the domes and minarets behind us on the Other Shore.
"Friend!" he exclaims, shaking my hand, embracing me. I
introduce my Beloved…

As if on the snowy peak of Mount Sumeru,
we're the axis of memories whirling away.

The Pickpocket

(Nameless as a pickpocket. Why should we be any different? In the evening, on the way back across the Bridge, a man wants to sell us postcards, exchange a few Euro coins—at a profit for us! But he short-changes the Poet and his Muse, as an ascendant civilization would. All the Poet keeps calculating is how much might have been: the vanished coins in Dollars Australian: "Equal to sixty pages of that two volume monograph, *Armenian Painters of the Ottoman Age*." The one that reproduced, if all other biographical documents were lost, only the Disappeared's signature.)

Afterword

Echolalia, *or an Interview with a Ghost*

— ...

— It has occurred to me that there were several moments that I would see as orientating the beginnings of this book. The first was as a consequence of the reading I'd been doing through my interest in the Portuguese 'Discoveries', as they call them, when I was interested to find out just what the ground was that was being staked out at the very beginning of Western imperialism. As one reads those texts, the various first-hand accounts and subsequent early histories, it's clear that in many ways the Portuguese as colonisers were taking over ground previously occupied by 'the Moors'. Who were these 'Moors'?

I was preoccupied by all this, these thoughts of the origin of global imperial expansion as the beginning of the West's successful expulsion of the Moors from Iberia, seeing Portugal and Spain's taking over of world—yes, the entire world was divided in half between the two powers by Pope Alexander I at Tordesillas. This would later be affirmed for me in another way when in Egypt I came to understand that the Mamluk— which means 'slave'—domination of trade from the East up the Red Sea collapsed once the Portuguese rounded the Cape of Good Hope. I saw the War Against Terror as something akin to this expansionism, too. In Lisbon one morning I passed a newspaper kiosk and saw an incredible photograph on the front page of several of the newspapers, a picture straight out of the Middle Ages, out of the Inquisition. It was one of those photographs taken by the US soldiers in Abu Ghraib Prison, of them 'sporting' with their prisoners. It also reminded me of some of those paintings Goya did of people in madhouses. I felt then, as I still do now, that the conflicts and political structures of the Middle Ages have more to teach us about what is going on today than the ideas of the Modern Era. So, there is the question of what role Islam and Arabic culture—the 'Moors'—have in all this, since the US and the Coalition of the Willing has so effectively remade them into enemies of the West. It might not be fair to put it like that because there was 9/11 and there have been attacks on the West other than in the US...

From a more literary perspective there's something else I should say. Just under ten years ago I spent some time in the US and was at various times, if only from the periphery, witness to their poetry scenes. I once had a conversation with the poet Susan Howe, at the home of the late Robert Creeley's wife, where I found myself explaining the circumstances I have 'emerged' from: that Afrikaans is my second language, a language that we in South Africa were compelled to learn under Apartheid, that its earliest texts were written by Muslim exiles in Cape Town; also that Portuguese was once the *lingua-franca* of the Indian Ocean; and that the grammar of South African English echoes Afrikaans. I told her, if I am recalling this correctly, that the tone of my English seems elusive for many readers and is better understood once the poems enter translation. It was also at that time that I was associating with some American translators of Spanish— partly because I found the American poetry world over-professionalised and theocratic, each practitioner believing her aesthetic is the One, and is neurotic for that. This led me to look at Latin American literature and to re-read a book I had only half-appreciated when I'd first read it many years before—Maria Rosa Menocal's *Shards of Love: Exile and the Origins of the Lyric*. Pity about the title because this is an extraordinary and strange book, arguing that Provençal poetry, the source of much of the poetics of the Romance languages, and the ideal of Romance itself with its notion of unrequited love, has its origins in a repression of the syncreticism that is to be found in the poetries of Iberia under the Moors. There were a few points she made that were of special interest to me and shaped my thinking about the poems that would become *Unbelievers*. She connects the expulsion of the Jews from Spain, the foundation of Castilian grammar and the nature of their heritage produced by interaction with the 'locals' and the occupying Muslims with the Spanish imperial entry into the Americas, and says that this is the background for the later flourishing cultures of Cuba and other parts of Latin America.

With my interest in Indonesia, that Islamic country just across the sea to the north of Australia, my feeling was that the Great South Land was an upside-down Iberia, that Indonesia was my Morocco, Africa my South America. And I knew, too, that there was a transnational, Indian Ocean Islamic tradition, which, in the case of Afrikaans, had some bearing on my own writing. This is something I have written about in poems about Cape Town, the city where my parents were born.

– …

– That is a very specific and interesting example. I had always wondered about the origin of that Apartheid term of abuse: 'kaffir'. A word that was made illegal, that has disappeared from public use. Who remembers those wars the British called the Kaffir Wars? Of course, the word is derived from the Arabic 'kafir', used to designate 'unbelievers', or those said to conceal the Truth. So how did it become that word, that harrowing insult from the mouths of those implementing Apartheid? How did a word that must have been used by Arabs against Africans, or rather I should say

Muslims against Africans, arrive in the Whiteman's Language?

For me, as a poet, as someone wanting to rid my language of violence, I thought I must return to contemplate what can be found in this strange, ghostly English I use, to find what represents Arabic vestige and what that poetics might be. Menocal had already shown me a way, particularly in her reflections on the poetic form of the *muwashah*, its linguistic impurity being the reason for the genre's exclusion from monolingual studies of Medieval Iberia. It must be said that the violence of that word 'kaffir', its induction of pain, is consistent with the fact that in East Africa and elsewhere in Africa there was a relation between Islam and the centuries-long enslavement of Africans from the inland areas.

– ...

– You could say I am interested in lost histories. I wouldn't really see it like that, but that is a way of describing my interests in *Unbelievers*. Certainly, Andalusia, the world of al'Andalus, is idealized in that way, as the lost possibility of an harmonious cohabitation of the West and Islam. I'm not sure how right that is. If it was so harmonious, why did the proto-Spanish and -Portuguese, under the flag of Christianity, drive the Moors out? The invasion of the rest of the globe may be seen as a continuation of the sweep of that successful expulsion. If you look at my poem 'After the only known poem by Abd al'Rahman', in my version a poem of exile written from Australia's far-flung West, it is clear that al'Rahman wishes he wasn't in Iberia, yearning rather for the metropolitan centres of Damascus or Baghdad, places we are now hearing from again as a consequence of the War Against Terror. But also it shouldn't be forgotten that al'Rahman may have been seen as what the news-media today would call a 'warlord'. In one of the battles in which he took over his part of Iberia he had the many thousands of defeated all beheaded. Are we in better or worse times? Donald Rumsfeld, that warlord, once wrote a ditty that he presented at a White House event as a poem, and this was publicly ridiculed by some US poets. But would we really be in a better world if he were able to write a poem as good as al'Rahman's?

I wouldn't think so much in terms of lost histories, rather in terms of histories that appear and disreappear, and histories that are influential even if invisible. The scholar Daniel Heller-Roazen's wonderful book *Echolalias: On the Forgetting of Language* is entirely about this in regard to language. His argument, if I may encapsulate it, is that languages are as much appearing as disappearing and that it isn't always clear where one language begins and another language ends, or even when a language has ended. In my case, it's not entirely clear where Afrikaans exits from Dutch and becomes another language. This is especially interesting in the relationship between nation and language or, as some of the Afrikaner nationalists put it, echoing the Nazis, between 'Land en Taal'. It was the Cape Malays, a community of deracinated people from various parts of the Indian Ocean world, a people lacking a common language, who used it as their own long before it became part of the project of Afrikaner nationalism.

In poetics this horizon of appearance and disappearance is key, too, in that in the Poem we always have at issue the poetic form and language itself. We have the material—the form—of how we think words should be composed to be a poem, and those words themselves, whether naturalized, loan- or foreign-words, all that elusive material. And, besides, both might come to us twinned in the media of sound or writing, with their own heritages and constraints of performance. In *Unbelievers* I sometimes take this literally. In the poem 'The Moor' I follow to a good extent the rules of the Andalusian *muwashah*, in form and theme. With today's political anxieties, that poem was immediately rejected by a editor-translator in Paris who'd solicited poems about the act of reading. I think he thought it was racist! It could, perhaps, be read in that way. But really I was writing a proper *muwashah*. The Galician woman referred to in the poem saw its irony and humour, and I, as an African of a kind, feel I should respond to the stereotyping of Africa.

If we are to talk about lost histories we should also talk about the position of Jewish culture and Hebrew in the book, even if that is only a small part of what is contemplated in the poems. My grandmother was Jewish and her father, a Lithuanian Jew, established one of Cape Town's synagogues. There are a few points at which this is touched on. There are references in the title of one poem to 'La Nacão', the name the Portuguese Jews in Amsterdam gave to themselves, and there is the sequence about Avraham ben Yitzhak, who readers of Elias Canetti's three-volume autobiography would know as a mysterious figure Canetti and others idolized. Yitzhak is an insightful example regarding the question of history and language, he being a man of the late nineteenth and early twentieth centuries, and typically multilingual. In his poetry, he writes in a Hebrew that shows the traces of the poetics of German Romanticism and the—let me use this expression—timeless language of Biblical Hebrew. Whether it was the tension of these languages or the trauma of his times that caused him to write only eleven poems, I don't know. I understand he is seen as an essential figure in the establishment of the contemporary Hebrew language, a language, of course, central to the notion of state in Israel. Heller-Roazen, makes the point that grammatically modern Hebrew owes a lot to German. In fact, he reminds us that when there was discussion over which language the Jewish state should have there was a strong case made for German as so many of the immigrants to the new country had abandoned Germany and Central Europe, and German is one of the components of Yiddish.

When I think on Yitzhak, I can't help thinking of Paul Celan, who produced in his poems a kind of anti-German, a transcendental—if I may use that word—non-language inside a brutalised one, a sacramental alternative as far as that is possible. I also think of Nelly Sachs, the important but lesser-known poet internationally, who corresponded with Celan and who was, it seems, a kind of mentor to him. I remember in Stockholm by chance passing her apartment building at the waterside. A few years later, seeing an exhibition about her life at the Jewish Museum in Berlin, I read again that she'd had a mental breakdown after hearing a particular Nazi-era phrase uttered when she'd gone to collect a prize in Switzerland.

To me, and this might surprise many of my readers, especially of a book that takes Islamic visage as its focus, Jewish modern history was often at the back of my mind, because the Jewish presence in South Africa, like the Portuguese, is substantial.

– …

– I don't really want to go into too much detail about the poems. 'Os Elefantes Brancos' are two poems about South Africa, about ex-whites, those 'white elephants', and the poems are as accurate as I could make them. What I would say is that, within the context of the rest of the book, and in relation to lost histories, with them I was trying to reclaim a greater sense of the reality of those people's experience—mine included— than is often presented. Often I am asked whether my name is Afrikaans. When I explain that it's not, I frequently discover that my interlocutor has assumed that all 'white' South Africans were Afrikaners. Also, there is sometimes the tacit assumption that all white South Africans were somehow either supporters of Apartheid or violently—it is strange to use that adjective here—opposed it. The complexity of living in those years isn't easy to explain today.

That story by Isaac Bashevis Singer that I refer to at the end of 'The Ex-Photographer' does give a sense of a certain lost history that one can intuit in Lisbon, of the history of the Jews, the *Conversos*, who continued to live there worshipping in secret after the Expulsion.

It must also be said, based on my experience, that for many people unfamiliar with South African history my sense of orientation might seem odd. To people from Cape Town, and remember both my parents were born there and two of my grandmothers, there was always a sense of cosmopolitanism, its being a port-city half way between the West and the East. Not that the complexity of its history is fully understood even today. When I gave a talk in Salzburg and mentioned the history of writing in the Cape Malay community and how it related to the various pre-colonial writing traditions existent in parts of what is now Indonesia, a student on exchange from Cape Town told me he had never heard anything along those lines at his university back in South Africa. Yes, invisible histories…

There is another aspect of this which has a bearing on my ethical aspirations for *Unbelievers*. Namely, that I see the War Against Terror, which is or isn't still going on, itself a now-visible-now-invisible phenomenon, with drones and eavesdropping, as a kind of continuing or echoing of the Cold War, and of the psychological structures of several centuries of interlocking imperialisms. Although I have thoughts on this and its connection to the violence required to sustain the particular and newly developed economic methods of global capitalism, on the way it needs to destroy those aspects of the pre-modern that have sustained 'undeveloped' societies for hundreds or thousands of years, I would prefer to restrict myself to remarking on what this means for the book. There is a range of poetry in this book, from the narratives of 'Os Elefantes Brancos' to the attenuated voicings of '(Twelve Poems)', 'Monsanto' and 'The Language'. 'The Language' was originally written in Afrikaans and has been translated into Farsi, and was privately distributed as a chapbook in Tehran. There are the lyrics, even a translated lyric about the Moorish part of Lisbon by the roaming Dutch poet, J Slauerhoff. What I hoped would unite them is a sense of the poems being, like Cape Town, halfway, whether between one culture and another, between one language and its translation, a kind of ghost-writing. Hence the frequent reference to translation, I suppose.

There is a metaphysic implicit in this, what I would characterise as a philosophy of the incomplete, of remains. A friend's bookshop in Lisbon, now in Rio de Janeiro, and referred to in one of my poems, is called—in Portuguese—Incomplete Poetry, when actually it probably has every

Portuguese poetry book you could think of! In this I may be introducing an Asian understanding of experience. Here I'm thinking of a book on Chinese painting, *The Great Image Has no Form, or On the Nonobject through Painting*, by François Jullien in which he explains the importance of incompleteness and space to the expression and depiction of Being. This, I sense, is why many of the poems are so much like miniatures, and this prevents the work from becoming statements, enactments, embodiments. I don't want to be in the situation where I 'proclaim'. There is a contradiction here, concerned as I am in some way with Islam, as one of the essential difficulties for Islam and Arab culture in its confrontation with modernity and the West, an argument put forward by the Syrian poet Adonis, is that of the central and timeless role of the Arabic language in *The Qu'ran*. The novelist J.M. Coetzee, speaking at a Cape Town event many years ago in what was intended to be a defence of Salman Rushdie and his book *The Satanic Verses*, a defence I imagine against radical figures of the city's Islamic community, made the point, to the consternation of some of the liberal-minded audience, that we need to think carefully about whether a modern book may be critical of a holy book, need to think about that because clearly those who believe in *The Qu'ran*, in this instance, don't. I mention this in one of the poems of 'Os Elefantes Brancos'.

Further, the Cold War effected the political discourse of South Africa such that the Apartheid government presented its policies as a war against Communism. Now that hardly anyone seems to talk about Communism in the West, except those who have a dream of a left-wing alternative to the all-consuming ideology of the new forms of global capitalism, talking about South Africa's covert war against Angola and Mozambique and the country's Cold War rhetoric, let alone the involvement of Britain, the US, Cuba and the Soviet Union, seems almost a science-fiction. Yet I think we must remember that there are people around us who did believe those things, just as we are now required to believe in globalism, and who did fight in those conflicts, coming home with the physical and mental wounds of war. It is possible to feel morally outraged at all this, but increasingly I feel that the structure of civilisation itself requires war, bloodshed and invasion.

For some years I have been working on a book-length poem about a South African veteran of the war against Angola, and the more I have tried to understand the psychological nature of war, the more I have seen its originary dynamics in the story of Abraham and Isaac. I disagree with

Kierkegaard in his *Fear and Trembling*, because for me the 'leap of faith' is only a belief in governance, whether actual or metaphysical. The more I've worked on that book, still thinking through the ideas of *Southern Barbarians*, my poems about the Portuguese empire, and about these poems related to our being 'unbelievers', the more I feel power is always trying either to defeat us or to hypnotise us. Good poems interfere with that.

– …

– I fear all these thoughts on historical and political questions are taking us away from thinking about the literary, the poetic. As I said before, my discovery of Menocal's book and her other work, and my investigating of the importance of the idea of the Baroque to Latin American literature, whether fiction or poetry, led me to look at the poems I'd written about Portugal in a different way. I started to see them as an expression of my own interest in an undeclared or possible Baroque, a Baroque of the Indian Ocean. And the other side of it was linguistic: there is the usually unremarked upon fact that at the edges of the known world it was Arabic that was expected to be the common language. Columbus, de Gama and even Zheng He, the Chinese admiral who was in command of a fleet that explored the Indian Ocean shortly before de Gama's arrival, who was himself a Muslim and said to be the founder of Malacca, had translators of that language with them on their voyages.

What does this mean for my poems? There are, at least, the points of orientation: Cede Hamede Benegeli is—according to Cervantes no less!— the author of the book *Don Quixote*; the untranslated graffiti on a wall in Lavapies, a cosmopolitan neighbourhood in Madrid known for its African population from the Muslim north, is in Galician, a language from the north-west of Spain and related to Portuguese; 'The Andalusian Poet' is a series of echoes of Lorca and his Afrikaans translator, the influential Uys Krige; and there is 'While in the Salon dos Embajadores…', written in Andalusia, at the place where Queen Isabella commissioned Columbus to sail in the direction of India, written some years after the lecture described, a lecture which I presented in the days following the attack on the World Trade Centre in New York and in which I read from Adonis' poem 'Death of New York', with its allusion to Lorca and images of people falling from buildings. There are the names named: Abd al'Rahaman, the travellers Ibn Battuta and Ibn Zunbul; the novelists J.M. Coetzee, Juan Goytisolo, Mia Couto, Amos Tutuola and Voltaire; the poets Helberto Helder, J Slauerhoff, Camilio Pessanha, Araham ben

Yitzhak; the South African photographer Santu Mofokeng and fifteenth-century Portuguese master painter known as Grão Vasco. All of them are part of a world that can come together in an almost invisible history. And we shouldn't forget, although he is only very briefly mentioned, but his work *The Ethics* is the subject of a sequence of my poems, some of which have appeared in magazines in Prague and London, the philosopher Baruch Spinoza, whose origin was Portuguese and Jewish and who now is mostly regarded as a Dutch—or should I say Western?—intellectual hero.

What I would like you to note is not all that, the arcane details of the references, that weird kind of erudition. What I think all these poems, the bulk of which written over seven or so years in Dubai, Lisbon, Coimbra, Monsanto, Cairo, Hurgharda, Istanbul, Munich, and various cities in Spain—although the earliest poem, 'The Language', in an Afrikaans version that is now lost, was written more than twenty years ago—should point to is, to use a term conventional in the contemporary art-world, 'historicity', especially historicity of tone. I have been following this path because, though I spoke English as my first language growing up in South Africa, it was in certain Afrikaans poets that I found the tone that I recognised as poetic. In those years there were no poets writing in English in South Africa or elsewhere that moved me. And when I started to try to understand why the poems of Eugène Marais or Breyten Breytenbach or Ingrid Jonker did touch me, I found that translation was involved: Marais often wrote in English, he the author of some of his language's most astonishing lyrics; Breytenbach and Jonker had the advantage of being the generation after the translator Uys Krige, an impressive figure whose work on French, Spanish and Latin American poetry had a decisive influence on subsequent Afrikaans poetry. My first published poems, as I understand it, struck readers as being atonal, and this is a serious issue in the British-influenced context of Australia where the laconic mode is the basis of its language. One critic has said that I seem a supranational poet, coming from nowhere. Another, in a speech at a book launch many years ago, paid me the curious complement of drawing a parallel between the tone of my poems and that of the Austrian expressionist Georg Trakl. He intended it a bit ironically, probably, but I think it could make sense in that Trakl's tone has an intense, one could say at the risk of being misunderstood, 'absolute' tone. Early on in my work I was reading Celan and a number of other German language poets as complementary to the Afrikaans.

It's this question of tone, though, that I would like to stress. What is it when a tone comes into one language from another, or from another poetry tradition? It could be that it usually meets with a deafness, the readers saying, "We can't hear the voice". There is also an interesting question of phenomenology here. On the other hand, it could be said that the history of literature is a history of the importing of techniques and tones from one language and one literary tradition to another. Menocal's example is a good one. But we could even say that much of Eliot's 'The Waste Land' owes its tone, its vocal techniques as well as its mood, to a certain stream of French poetry. In my poem 'The Language' a like mutation takes place. I was seeking a particular tone in the Afrikaans original, which was itself, I would say, derived from the Arabic—maybe even the Persian—influence on Spanish poetry that came to Afrikaans through Krige's translations. By translating the poem into English, into my so-called atonality, I was able to present it to a Farsi translator, who, through her translation, returned it, perhaps, to its point of origin such that readers in today's Tehran said that to them it sounded like a Farsi poem, moreover like a poem by a particular modern Iranian poet. It's true that that poem, that translation, may be anomalous, may not be 'strong' in the English… Or, maybe we should say that to hear the poem well in English you need to hear it as translation?

– …

– No, this interest in tone is not, if I understood you correctly, only a literary quality. Tone is something sonic, physical, psychological, suggestive of mood and the relationship between the speaker and the listener, and of tradition, of a psychology, that which isn't necessarily disclosed. So while tone has been a focus of literary criticism it is always an elemental aspect of utterance. And what I've been observing in the teaching of poetry that I've done occasionally over the past decade is that the students, quite often even the academics, don't feel they need to attend to tone. This an aspect of a fear of the emotional and the personal, a fear of the honesty that is required to pay attention that is typical of our kind of Western capitalist logic. With this book I am hoping, in one way at least, to introduce this idea that we need to imagine tones we can't quite hear, that we should acknowledge, too, how partial our sense of reality is. We easily imagine, for example, that Western culture is coherent, that there are 'objects of interest' that are inside the system and likewise others that are outside, but maybe we shouldn't, or can't, tell the inside from the outside? Maybe a Persian notion of love is what has driven the poetries of the Romance languages, and that the object of love sought in the Beloved of the Troubadour poets was a Sufi's Allah?

With language itself, maybe we are wrong in thinking we are inside our language, and that we can speak our language because we know it? Maybe our languages, in their implicit, continuing incompleteness, are a kind of echololia, that echoing a child makes when all phonemes are possible, when a child is trying out the purest materials of language? Maybe a book like *Unbelievers* can be a reminder of the extent to which every utterance is an occasion, a moment of connection, however fragmentary, before we fall back again united in the Void?

(Lisbon, June 2013)

www.ingramcontent.com/pod-product-compliance
Lightning Source LLC
Chambersburg PA
CBHW031147160426
43193CB00008B/280